MEDITATING
ON THE
PROMISES OF GOD

KATIE M. LITTLES

THE WRITE
LEGACY

MEDITATING

on the

Promises of God

By Katie M. Littles

Copyright © 2020 by Katie M. Littles

All rights reserved. No part of this book may be reproduced or used in any manner without written permission of the copyright owner except for the use of quotations in a book review.

Scriptures marked KJV are taken from the KING JAMES VERSION (KJV): KING JAMES VERSION, public domain.
Scriptures marked NIV are taken from the NEW INTERNATIONAL VERSION (NIV): Scripture taken from THE HOLY BIBLE, NEW INTERNATIONAL VERSION ®. Copyright© 1973, 1978, 1984, 2011 by Biblica, Inc.™. Used by permission of Zondervan

Scriptures marked NLT are taken from the HOLY BIBLE, NEW LIVING TRANSLATION (NLT): Scriptures taken from the HOLY BIBLE, NEW LIVING TRANSLATION, Copyright© 1996, 2004, 2007 by Tyndale House Foundation. Used by permission of Tyndale House Publishers, Inc., Carol Stream, Illinois 60188. All rights reserved. Used by permission.

Scriptures marked AMP are taken from the AMPLIFIED BIBLE (AMP): Scripture taken from the AMPLIFIED® BIBLE, Copyright © 1954,

1958, 1962, 1964, 1965, 1987 by the Lockman Foundation Used by Permission. (www.Lockman.org)

Scripture taken from The Message. Copyright Â© 1993, 1994, 1995, 1996, 2000, 2001, 2002. Used by permission of NavPress Publishing Group.

Scripture quotations taken from the New American Standard Bible® (NASB),

Copyright © 1960, 1962, 1963, 1968, 1971, 1972, 1973,

1975, 1977, 1995 by The Lockman Foundation

Used by permission. www.Lockman.org

Published by: The Write Legacy LLC Printed in the United States of America

ISBN: 9781734859201
ISBN-13: 978-1-7348592-0-1

www.thewritelegacypublishing@gmail.com

DEDICATION

This book is dedicated to my grandmother, Katie Mae Byrd. A woman of great strength and courage. Although she experienced great adversity, she remained strong and trusted God to the end.

Keep resting in heaven Mama. You're forever in my heart.

MED'ITATE, verb intransitive [Latin meditor; Spanish meditar; French mediter.]

1. To dwell on any thing in thought; to contemplate; to study; to turn or revolve any subject in the mind; appropriately but not exclusively used of pious contemplation, or a consideration of the great truths of religion.

His delight is in the law of the Lord, and in his law doth he meditate day and night. Psalm 1.

(Webster, Noah. American Dictionary of the English Language (1828 Edition) (Kindle Locations 177529-177532). Packard Technologies. Kindle Edition.)

How to Use this Book

The Bible is filled with hundreds, if not thousands, of promises from God. The promises on the following pages are just a fraction of what God has for those who believe. Although small, *Meditating on the Promises of God* is not meant to be a quick read. Take your time and mull over each scripture and Questions to Ponder until you get a good understanding of each promise and make notes in the space provided. There are several ways you can use this book:

(1) Read a passage a day, preferably in the morning so you can meditate (think about) it throughout the day.

(2) Stay on one passage for multiple days. Like I said earlier, this book isn't meant to be a quick read.

(3) The passages are not placed in any particular order; randomly pick a passage and meditate on it. I pray that *Meditating on the Promises of God* will be a catalyst for you to seek all of God's promises.

Meditating on the Promises of God is set up as follows:

1. The Focus Scripture

This is a promise found in God's Word. It's the main passage of scripture you will be meditating on. Read it silently a few times and read it out loud a few times.

2. Thoughts to Ponder

Questions or thoughts to consider after reading the focus scripture.

3. See Also

Additional scriptures to help reinforce the concept or truth of the focus scripture.

4. Confession

A suggested way to verbally confess the focus scripture for yourself.

5. My Thoughts

This is space for you to write what the focus scripture means to you. As your relationship with God deepens, He will begin to give you even more revelation of His truth.

You may notice many of the same scriptures are referenced repeatedly; this wasn't done on purpose, but it does show that the Bible is God's authoritative Word and how interconnected The Old and New Testaments are.

All scripture is from the King James Version (KJV) unless noted otherwise.

Jeremiah 29:11 (NIV)

"For I know the plans I have for you", declares the Lord, "plans to prosper you and not to harm you, plans to give you hope and a future".

Thoughts to Ponder:

- God already has plans for my life.
- God wants me to be successful.
- God does not want to harm me.

Also See:

Job 8:7; Lamentations 3:26; Isaiah 46:10-11

Confession:

God knows the plans He has for me; plans to prosper me and not to hurt me. He has plans to give me a hope and a future.

Meditating on the Promises of God

My Thoughts:

Psalm 139:14

I praise You, for I am fearfully and wonderfully made. Marvelous are Your works, and I know this very well.

Thoughts to Ponder:

- I am made in a manner to impress admiration and astonishment.
- I am made in a manner to excite wonder or surprise.
- God's works are wonderful and strange; they excite some degree of surprise.

Also See:

Genesis 1:26-27; Psalm 92:4-5; Psalm 104; Psalm 111:2

Confession:

I praise God because I am fearfully and wonderfully made. God's works are marvelous, and my soul knows that right well!

My Thoughts:

Romans 8:28

And we know that God works all things together for the good for those who love Him, who are the called according to His purpose.

Thoughts to Ponder:

- God will use the undesirable situations in our life to give Him glory.
- I love God.
- I am the called according to God's purpose.

Also See:

Genesis 50:20; 1 John 4:10; 1 John 5:2-3

Confession:

All things work together for my good because I love God and am called according to His purpose.

Meditating on the Promises of God

My Thoughts:

Genesis 1:26-27

26Then God said, "Let Us make man in Our image, after Our likeness, to rule over the fish of the sea and the birds of the air, over the livestock, and over all the earth itself and every creature that crawls upon it. 27 So God created man in His own image; in the image of God He created him; male and female He created them."

Thoughts to Ponder:

- I am produced by God from God, Jesus, and the Holy Spirit.
- I resemble God's character.
- I have authority and power.

Also See:

Psalm 100:3; Ephesians 4:24; John 1:1-14

Confession:

I am created in the image and likeness of God, Jesus, and the Holy Spirit

My Thoughts:

Joshua 1:9

Have I not commanded thee? Be strong and of a good courage; be not afraid, neither be thou dismayed: for the LORD thy God is with thee whithersoever thou goest.

Thoughts to Ponder:

- God requires that I am strong and courageous. He is always with me.
- I am able to sustain attacks because I am firmly planted in God's Word.
- I am not impressed with fear nor am I disheartened.

Also See:

Genesis 28:15; Jeremiah 1:7-8; Psalm 46:7

Confession:

I am strong and very courageous. I am not afraid; I am not discouraged, for the LORD my God is with me wherever I go.

Meditating on the Promises of God

My Thoughts:

Joshua 24:15

And if it seem evil unto you to serve the LORD, choose you this day whom ye will serve; whether the gods which your fathers served that were on the other side of the flood, or the gods of the Amorites, in whose land ye dwell: but as for me and my house, we will serve the LORD.

Thoughts to Ponder:

- I will not live my life according to traditions passed down through generations that don't align with God's Word.
- My environment will not determine my beliefs and actions.
- I choose to serve God.

Also See:

Genesis 18:19; Exodus 23:32-33; John 6:67-68

Confession:

But as for me and my house, we will serve the LORD.

My Thoughts:

_____

_____

_____

_____

_____

_____

_____

Isaiah 54:17

No weapon that is formed against thee shall prosper; and every tongue that shall rise against thee in judgement thou shalt condemn. This is the heritage of the servants of the LORD, and their righteousness is of me, saith the LORD.

Thoughts to Ponder:

- Neither people nor things that come to annoy, distract, or destroy me will be successful.
- When people form untrue opinions or speak untruths about or to me, I will prove them to be wrong through my actions and reactions.
- My righteousness is of God.

Also See:

Isaiah 54:15; John 10: 28-30; Romans 8:28-39; 2 Corinthians 5:21

Confession:

No weapon formed against me shall prosper; and I shall condemn every tongue that rises against me in judgement. This is my heritage because I am a servant of the LORD, and my righteousness is of God, says the LORD.

My Thoughts:

_____

_____

_____

_____

_____

2 Timothy 1:7

For God hath not given us the spirit of fear; but of power, and of love, and of a sound mind.

Thoughts to Ponder:

- Fear is a state of mind.
- Fear is false evidence appearing real (author unknown).
- Fear is a weapon used by the enemy to stop me from doing what God wants me to do.

Also See:

Proverbs 2:7; Luke 10:19; John 14:27; Romans 5:5; 2 Corinthians 5:13-14; 1 John 4:18; 1 Corinthians 2:16

Confession:

I don't have the spirit of fear. I have the spirit of love. I have the spirit of power. I have good will toward all men, I have the ability to do the things I need to do, I think and comprehend clearly.

Meditating on the Promises of God

My Thoughts:

Philippians 4:13

I can do all things through Christ who gives me strength.

Thoughts to Ponder:

- I don't have to do anything in my own strength.
- Christ confirms and establishes me and causes me to increase in power.
- When I acknowledge God in what I'm doing, He guides me.

Also See:

Zechariah 4:6; Isaiah 40:29-31; Isaiah 41:10; Proverbs 3:5-6; Ephesians 6:10; John 15:4-7; 2 Corinthians 3:4-5

Confession:

I can do all things through Christ who strengthens me.

My Thoughts:

Psalm 1:3

And he shall be like a tree planted by the rivers of water, that bringeth forth his fruit in his season; his leaf also shall not wither, and whatsoever he doeth shall prosper.

Thoughts to Ponder:

Trees serve and protect
1. They shade and cool the air and the stream water. It's what they're known for.
2. Trees actually can clean the soil and the water percolating through it by absorbing chemicals and other pollutants. Scientists have studied how trees filter sewage and farm chemicals, reduce the harmful effects of concentrated animal wastes, and clean water runoff that enters streams.
3. Trees slow stormwater runoff and reduce the threat of flooding.
4. Trees break the force of wind to help keep topsoil in place. Their roots bind the soil contributing to bank stabilization.

5. Trees create oxygen. A mature tree produces as much oxygen in a growing season as 10 people inhale in a year. They also act as giant filters cleaning the air we breathe. Trees clean the air by intercepting airborne particles, reducing heat and absorbing pollutants such as carbon monoxide, sulfur dioxide and nitrogen dioxide.
6. When they grow old and die, logs that have fallen into a stream will make great habitat for fish.

https://northsantiam.org/six-good-reasons-to-plant-trees-beside-a-strea/

There's an appointed time for the fruit of your labor to be shown to the world.

Also See:

Genesis 39:23; Jeremiah 17:8; Ezekiel 47:12; 2 Chronicles 31:21

Confession:

I am like the tree planted by the rivers of water. I bring forth my fruit in my season; my leaf also shall not wither; and everything I do shall prosper.

My Thoughts:

2 Corinthians 12:9

And He said unto me, My grace is sufficient for thee: for My strength is made perfect in weakness. Most gladly therefore will I rather glory in my infirmities, that the power of Christ may rest upon me.

Thoughts to Ponder:

- Grace is the empowering presence of God that enables me to do what He has called me to do, to be what He has called me to be, and to have all that He says I will have (Apostle Jerome Dukes)
- When I acknowledge my weaknesses, God is then able to support me completely and give me clear direction and guidance

Also See:

Proverbs 3:5-7; 1 Thessalonians 5:18; Zechariah 4:6; Philippians 4:13; 2 Corinthians 12:10

Confession:

God's grace is enough for me; His strength is made perfect in my weakness. Most gladly therefore will I rather glory in my infirmities, that the power of Christ may rest upon me.

My Thoughts:

Nehemiah 8:10

Then he said unto them, Go your way, eat the fat, and drink the sweet, and send portions unto them for whom nothing is prepared: for this day is holy unto our LORD: neither be ye sorry; for the joy of the LORD is your strength.

Thoughts to Ponder:

- Conviction brings remorsefulness.
- When we recognize and turn from our sin, God is pleased; this brings Him joy.
- God's joy is my strength.

Also See:

2 Chronicles 7:14-16; Isaiah 61:10; Romans 8:1

Confession:

This day is holy unto my LORD. The joy of the LORD is my strength.

Katie M. Littles

My Thoughts:

Deuteronomy 31:6

Be strong and of a good courage, fear not, nor be afraid of them: for the LORD thy God, He it is that doth go with thee; He will not fail thee, nor forsake thee.

Thoughts to Ponder:

- Courage begins in my heart.
- Fear is an emotion when I see false evidence that appears to be real.
- God will not abandon me, nor will He quit on me.

Also See:

Ephesians 6:10; Psalm 27:14; 1 Chronicles 22:13

Confession:

I am strong and courageous. I do not fear nor am I in dread because the LORD my God will never leave me nor forsake me.

Katie M. Littles

My Thoughts:

1 Peter 4:8

Above all, keep fervent in your love for one another, because love covers a multitude of sins.
(NASB)

Thoughts to Ponder:

- God and Jesus showed the ultimate act of love when Jesus died on the cross for my sins.
- How would I feel if God told everyone every sin I committed?
- When I have genuine good will towards others (no matter who they are or what they do) then it's easy for me to not expose their sin to the world.

Also See:

Proverbs 10:12; Proverbs 17:9; Colossians 3:14

Confession:

Above all, I am fervent in my love for others because love conceals a multitude of sin.

My Thoughts:

Proverbs 18:21

Death and life are in the power of the tongue and they that love it shall eat the fruit thereof.

Thoughts to Ponder:

- The words I speak have the ability to cause someone or something to live or to die.
- My thoughts determine what words come out of my mouth.
- Just because I think it, doesn't mean I should speak it.
- Spoken words cannot be taken back.

Also See:

Job 22:28; Proverbs 15:2-4; Matthew 12:36-37; Ephesians 4:29; James 1:19

Confession:

Death and life are in the power of the tongue; I choose to speak life.

My Thoughts:

Ephesians 4:29

Let no corrupt communication process out of your mouth, but that which is good to the use of edifying, that it may minister grace unto the hearers.

Thoughts to Ponder:

- My mouth is an instrument to be used to build and uplift others.
- When I speak, I am imparting something to others.
- My words plant seeds in those that hear them.

Also See:

Psalm 37:30-31; Proverbs 10:31-32; Colossians 3:8-9; Colossians 3:16-17

Confession:

I let no corrupt communication proceed from my mouth; only that which is good to the use of edifying, that it may minister grace (empowerment) unto the hearers.

My Thoughts:

_____

_____

_____

_____

_____

_____

_____

2 Corinthians 5:7

(For we walk by faith, not by sight:)

Thoughts to Ponder:

- Faith is the substance of things hoped for and the evidence of things not seen.
- Faith is believing something good will happen even though my circumstances say otherwise.
- Faith is the opposite of fear.

Also See:

Romans 10:17; Hebrews 10:38; Hebrews 11:1; Hebrews 11:6; 2 Corinthians 4:18

Confession:

I walk by faith and not by sight.

My Thoughts:

Meditating on the Promises of God

Deuteronomy 28:3-9

³ Blessed shalt thou be in the city, and blessed shalt thou be in the field. ⁴ Blessed shall be the fruit of thy body, and the fruit of thy ground, and the fruit of thy cattle, the increase of thy kine, and the flocks of thy sheep. ⁵ Blessed shall be thy basket and thy store. ⁶ Blessed shalt thou be when thou comest in, and blessed shalt thou be when thou goest out.
7 The LORD shall cause thine enemies that rise up against thee to be smitten before thy face: they shall come out against thee one way, and flee before thee seven ways. ⁸ The LORD shall command the blessing upon thee in thy storehouses, and in all that thou settest thine hand unto; and he shall bless thee in the land which the LORD thy God giveth thee. ⁹ The LORD shall establish thee an holy people unto himself, as he hath sworn unto thee, if thou shalt keep the commandments of the LORD thy God, and walk in his ways.

Thoughts to Ponder:

- God empowers me to prosper.
- God has given me dominion over everything He created.
- I always win when I follow God's instructions.

Also See:

Genesis 26:12; Exodus 19:5-6; Deuteronomy 26:18-19; Leviticus 26:4-5; Leviticus 26:7-8; Leviticus 26:10; Deuteronomy 15:10; Joshua 1:8; Joshua 10:42; Proverbs 3:9-10; Proverbs 10:22; Psalm 121:8; 2 Chronicles 1:10; Isaiah 1:19; Malachi 3:10-11; Luke 11:28; 1 Peter 2:9-11; 1 Peter 5:10

Confession:

I am empowered to prosper in the city. I am empowered to prosper in the field. My children are empowered to prosper. I am empowered to prosper when I come in and I am empowered to prosper when I go out. The LORD causes all the enemies

Meditating on the Promises of God

who rise up against me to be defeated before me. The LORD commands the blessings upon my home and all that I do.

My Thoughts:

Psalm 112:1-3 (NLT)

1 Praise the Lord! How joyful are those who fear the Lord and delight in obeying His commands. 2 Their children will be successful ever where, an entire generation of godly people. 3 They themselves will be wealthy, and their good deeds will last forever.

Thoughts to Ponder:

- To fear God means to reverence (respect, honor, obey) Him.
- My relationship with God determines how much joy I have, not my circumstances.
- The success and prosperity of my children are linked to my obedience to God.

Also See:

Psalm 1:1-2; Psalm 111:10; Psalm 145:19; Luke 1:50; Romans 7:22

Confession:

I am blessed because I fear the Lord and I delight greatly in His commandments. My children are successful upon the earth: they are blessed because they are the generation of the upright. Wealth and riches are in my house and my good deeds will last forever.

My Thoughts:

2 Corinthians 5:21

For He hath made Him to be sin for us, who knew no sin; that we might be made the righteousness of God through Him.

Thoughts to Ponder:

- I am in right standing with God because Jesus, the Christ (the Anointed One), paid the price for my sin.
- When God looks at me, He looks at me through the Blood of Jesus.
- My righteousness (outside of Jesus) is as filthy rags.

Also See:

Isaiah 53:4-6; Isaiah 64:6; John 3:16; Romans 5:17; Romans 10:3-4; 1 Corinthians 1:30; 1 Peter 3:18

Confession:

I am the righteousness of God through Christ Jesus.

Meditating on the Promises of God

My Thoughts:

Psalm 118:6

The Lord is on my side; I will not fear: what can man do unto me?

Thoughts to Ponder:

- God will never leave me nor forsake me.
- I trust God.
- All things work together for my good.

Also See:

Psalm 27:1-3; Jeremiah 20:11; Isaiah 51:12; Romans 8:28-39; Hebrews 13:6

Confession:

The Lord is on my side. I will not fear: what can man do unto me?

Meditating on the Promises of God

My Thoughts:

Matthew 5:44

But I say unto you, Love your enemies, bless them that curse you, do good to them that hate you, and pray for them which despitefully use you, and persecute you.

Thoughts to Ponder:

- Showing love (goodwill) towards my enemies is a testament of my love for God.
- Showing love (goodwill) towards my enemies might be the seed or water used by God to bring that person or persons into the Kingdom of God.

Also See:

Exodus 23:4-5; Proverbs 25:21-22; Luke 6:34-35; Romans 12:14; Romans 12:20-21; 1 Peter 2:23; 1 Peter 3:9

Confession:

I love my enemies, I bless those that curse me, I do good to them that hate me, and I pray for them that despitefully use me, and persecute me.

My Thoughts:

2 Timothy 2:15

Study to shew thyself approved unto God, a workman that needed not to be ashamed, rightly dividing the word of truth.

Thoughts to Ponder:

- When I set my heart to please God, I won't be ashamed.
- When I study God's Word, I ask Him for understanding and revelation.
- When God gives me understanding and revelation of His Word, I won't take it out of context or use it to justify my actions.

Also See:

Proverbs 3:5-7; Galatians 1:10; 1 Thessalonians 2:4; 2 Peter 1:10; 2 Corinthians 10:18

Confession:

I study to show myself approved unto God. I am a workman that is not ashamed, and I rightly divide the Word of Truth.

My Thoughts:

Isaiah 41:13

For I the Lord thy God will hold thy right hand, saying unto thee, Fear not, I will help thee.

Thoughts to Ponder:

- God is my Father and wants to help (sustain, support) me.
- Just as earthly parents look after and keep their children safe; God desires to do the same thing for me.
- The right hand is usually the stronger, more dominant hand. If God wants to hold my stronger hand, that lets me know that no matter how strong or capable I think I am, I can still use His help.

Also See:

Psalm 27:1; Isaiah 41:10; Isaiah 42:6; 2 Timothy 4:17

Confession:

The Lord my God holds my right hand, saying unto me, Fear not, I will help thee.

My Thoughts:

Isaiah 41:10

Fear thou not; for I am with thee: be not dismayed; for I am thy God: I will strengthen thee: yea, I will help thee; yea, I will uphold thee with the right hand of My righteousness.

Thoughts to Ponder:

- Fear is false evidence appearing real.
- Fear is a strategy the devil uses to keep me from moving forward.
- If God has told me to do a thing, He will make sure I have all I need to complete the assignment.

Also See:

Deuteronomy 31:6-8; Joshua 1:9; 2 Chronicles 20:17; Psalm 27:1; Psalm 46:7; Isaiah 40:29-31; Isaiah 43:1-2; Isaiah 51: 12-13; Romans 8:31; Philippians 4:13

Confession:

I don't fear because God is with me; I am not dismayed because God is my God, He strengthens me. Yes, He helps me! He upholds me with the right hand of His righteousness.

My Thoughts:

Deuteronomy 8:18

But thou shalt remember the LORD thy God: for it is He that giveth thee power to get wealth, that He may establish His covenant which He sware unto thy fathers, as it is this day.

Thoughts to Ponder:

- Power is the ability to do work.
- God doesn't give me the wealth; He gives me the ability and the wisdom to get the wealth.
- God established His covenant with Abraham, and I am Abraham's seed.

Also See:

Genesis 12:1-3; Deuteronomy 7:8; 1 Samuel 2:7; 2 Chronicles 25:9; Proverbs 8:12; Proverbs 10:22; Psalm 127:1-2; Galatians 3:29

Confession:

I remember the LORD my God because He gives me the power to get wealth, so that He can establish His covenant which He sware unto my ancestors.

My Thoughts:

Joshua 1:8

This book of the law shall not depart out of thy mouth; but thou shalt meditate therein day and night, that thou mayest observe to do according to all that is written therein: for then thou shalt make thy way prosperous, and then thou shalt have good success.

Thoughts to Ponder:

- God's Word gives me wisdom.
- God's Word tells me who I am.
- God's Word guides me.

Also See:

Deuteronomy 6:6-9; Deuteronomy 11:18-19; Deuteronomy 29:9; Psalm 1:1-3; Psalm 19:14; Psalm 119:15; Matthew 7:24; John 24:21; James 1:22-25; Colossians 3:16

Confession:

My way is prosperous, and I have good success because I meditate on God's Word day and night and I observe to do according to all that is written in it.

My Thoughts:

Psalm 91:1-2

1 He that dwelleth in the secret place of the Most High shall abide under the shadow of The Almighty. 2 I will say of the LORD, He is my refuge and my fortress: my God; in Him will I trust.

Thoughts to Ponder:

- My secret place in God is only known to Him and me.
- God's shadow conceals and protects me from danger.
- God is my shelter and protection from danger.

Also See:

Deuteronomy 33:27-29; Proverbs 18:10; Psalm 18:2; Psalm 27:5; Psalm 31:20; Psalm 32:7; Psalm 36:7; Psalm 46:1; Psalm 62:5-8; Isaiah 12:2; Isaiah 26:3-4

Confession:

I dwell in the secret place of The Most High and I abide under the shadow of The Almighty. God is my refuge and my fortress. In Him will I trust.

My Thoughts:

Psalm 118:17 (NASB)

I will not die but live and tell of the works of the Lord.

Thoughts to Ponder:

- I will not be deprived of anything God has already ordained for me.
- I will actively pursue (seek) God's face for His will for my life.
- I will make the works of God known through my actions and words.

Also See:

Psalm 40:5; Psalm 40:10; Psalm 73:28; Psalm 107:22

Confession:

I shall not die. I shall live and declare the works of the LORD.

My Thoughts:

Psalm 23:1-6

1 The LORD is my shepherd; I shall not want. 2 He makes me to lie down in green pastures: He leads me beside the still waters. 3 He restores my soul: He leads me in the paths of righteousness for His name's sake. 4 Yea, though I walk through the valley of the shadow of death, I will fear no evil: for Thou are with me; Thy rod and Thy staff they comfort me. 5 Thou prepares a table before me in the presence of my enemies: Thou anoints my head with oil; my cup runs over. 6 Surely goodness and mercy shall follow me all the days of my life: and I will dwell in the house of the LORD forever.

Thoughts to Ponder:

- The Shepherd (God) loves and takes care of all who belongs to Him. As long as I rely on the Shepherd, I don't lack anything.
- Green pastures = Prosperity and Success
- Still waters = Peace, Rest, Refreshing, and Renewal

Also See:

Psalm 46:4; Isaiah 30:23; Isaiah 41:10; Isaiah 42:16; Isaiah 43:1-2; Philippians 4:19; John 10:11; Acts 18:9-10; Psalm 45:7; John 10:9-10; Psalm 27:4; 2 Timothy 4:18

Confession:

The LORD is my caretaker. I don't lack anything. He makes me lay down in prosperous places. He leads me in peace. He restores my soul. He leads me in the right path for His name's sake. Even when I walk in places that seem to be scary, I don't fear because God is with me. His rod and His staff comforts me. God prepares great places for me in front of my enemies. He anoints my head with oil. My cup overflows. Surely grace and mercy follows me all the days of my life and I will live in the house of the LORD forever.

Katie M. Littles

My Thoughts:

Galatians 6:9

And let us not be weary in well doing: for in due season we shall reap, if we faint not.

Thoughts to Ponder:

- I operate in a place of well doing when what I do is in obedience to God.
- My times of well doing is also my time of sowing seeds.
- In God's timing my seed will produce a harvest of crops.
- Remember your why.

Also See:

Leviticus 26:4; Psalm 104:27; Isaiah 40:31; 1 Corinthians 3:11-13; 1 Corinthians 15:58; 2 Corinthians 9:6; Hebrews 12:3; James 5:7

Confession:

I am not weary in well doing. I reap in due season (God's timing) because I don't faint.

My Thoughts:

Isaiah 40:31 (NLT)

But those who trust in the LORD will find new strength. They will soar high on wings like eagles. They will run and not grow weary. They will walk and not faint.

Thoughts to Ponder:

- As I trust God, He will empower, strengthen, and refresh me.
- As I trust God, I will be able to do things I never thought were possible.
- God will cause me to rise above the storms of life and keep moving as long as I trust Him.

Also See:

Lamentations 3:25-26; Psalm 27:13-14; Psalm 103:1-5; Hebrews 12:1-2; Galatians 6:9; 1 Corinthians 2:9

Confession:

I find new strength because I trust in the LORD. I soar high on wings like eagles. I run and don't get weary. I walk and I don't faint.

My Thoughts:

Matthew 19:26

But Jesus beheld them, and said unto them, With man this is impossible; but with God all things are possible.

Thoughts to Ponder:

- God will do what I cannot do.
- Obstacles are opportunities for God to move.
- When I am weak, God is strong.

Also See:

Genesis 18:14; Numbers 11:23; Psalm 62:11; Jeremiah 32:17; Mark 10:27; Luke 1:37; Luke 18:27

Confession:

With God all things are possible.

Katie M. Littles

My Thoughts:

Romans 12:1-2

1I beseech you therefore, brethren, by the mercies of God, that ye present your bodies a living sacrifice, holy, and acceptable unto God, which is your reasonable service. 2And be not conformed to this world: be ye transformed by the renewing of your mind, that ye may prove what is that good, and acceptable, and perfect will of God.

Thoughts to Ponder:

- When something is transformed, it looks and functions different than it did before the transformation occurred.
- As a living sacrifice, I am dedicated to the service of the LORD.
- Only by applying God's Word to my life, I can present my body as a living sacrifice and I can prove what is the good, and acceptable, and perfect will of God.

Also See:

Romans 6:13; Ephesians 4:1; Ephesians 4:22-24; 1 Peter 2:10-12; 2 Corinthians 5:17; Titus 3:5

Confession:

I present my body a living sacrifice, holy, acceptable to God, this is my reasonable service. I am not conformed to this world. I have been transformed because I renew my mind through God's Word, so that I may prove what is the good, and acceptable, and perfect will of God.

My Thoughts:

James 1:2-4 (NLT)

2 Dear brothers and sisters, when troubles of any kind come your way, consider it an opportunity for great joy. 3 For you know that when your faith is tested, your endurance had a chance to grow. 4 So let it grow, for when your endurance is fully developed, you will be perfect and complete, needing nothing.

Thoughts to Ponder:

- Growth is a process.
- Troubles and challenges come to test you on what you know.
- Challenges help me grow.

Also See:

Matthew 5:10-12; Luke 6:22-23; 1 Peter 1:6-8; James 1:12; Romans 5:3-4; Colossians 1:11; Hebrews 10:36; Hebrews 12:1; 2 Corinthians 4:17; Romans 8:28; James 1:4; 1 Peter 5:10; Galatians 6:9

Confession:

When troubles of any kind come my way, I consider it an opportunity for great joy because when my faith is tested my endurance has a chance to grow. When my endurance is fully developed, I will be perfect and complete, needing nothing.

My Thoughts:

Mark 11:22-26

***22** And Jesus answering saith unto them, Have faith in God. **23** For verily I say unto you, That whosoever shall say unto this mountain, Be thou removed, and be thou cast into the sea; and shall not doubt in his heart, but shall believe that those things which he saith shall come to pass; he shall have whatsoever he saith. **24** Therefore I say unto you, What things soever ye desire, when ye pray, believe that ye receive them, and ye shall have them. **25** And when ye stand praying, forgive, if ye have ought against any: that your Father also which is in heaven may forgive you your trespasses. **26** But if ye do not forgive, neither will your Father which is in heaven forgive your trespasses.*

Thoughts to Ponder:

- Faith is the substance of things hoped for and the evidence of things not seen.
- If I don't have faith, I can't please God.
- The words I speak determine what I receive.
- Unforgiveness fuels anger, resentment, and hatred.
- None of these are attributes of God.

Also See:

Psalm 37:4; Matthew 6:12; Matthew 6:14-15; Matthew 17:20; Mark 9:23; Luke 6:37; Luke 17:6; John 15:7; John 14:13; Colossians 3:12-14; Ephesians 4:32; James 1:5-6; 1 John 5:14-15

Confession:

I have faith in God. When I pray, I don't doubt in my heart. I believe I receive those things I desire and what I desire shall come to pass. I forgive those who have offended me because God has forgiven me.

My Thoughts:

Meditating on the Promises of God

Ephesians 6:10-18

***10** Finally, my brethren, be strong in the Lord, and in the power of His might. **11** Put on the whole armour of God, that ye may be able to stand against the wiles of the devil. **12** For we wrestle not against flesh and blood, but against principalities, against powers, against the rulers of the darkness of this world, against the spiritual wickedness in high places. **13** Wherefore take unto you the whole armour of God, that ye may be able to withstand in the evil day and having done all to stand. **14** Stand therefore, having your loins girt about with truth, and having on the breastplate of righteousness. **15** And your feet shod with the preparation of the gospel of peace; **16** Above all, taking the shield of faith, wherewith ye shall be able to quench the fiery darts of the wicked. **17** And take the helmet of salvation, and the sword of the Spirit, which is the Word of God: **18** Praying always with all prayer and supplication in the Spirit and watching thereunto with all perseverance and supplication for all saints.*

Thoughts to Ponder:

- The battles I face are spiritual therefore, I must use spiritual weapons to fight them.
- I must speak those things that align with God's Word.
- I must do what is right in God's eyes.
- I must be peaceable with everyone.
- My faith is built up by hearing God's Word.

Also See:

Deuteronomy 20:3-4; Joshua 1:9; Psalm 56:3-4; Isaiah 11:1-5; Isaiah 40:31; Isaiah 52:7; Isaiah 59:16-17; Matthew 4:4; Luke 12:35; Luke 21:36; Acts 12:5; Philippians 4:6; Philippians 4:13; 2 Corinthians 2:10-11; 2 Corinthians 4:4; 2 Corinthians 10:4; 1 Peter 4:7; 1 Peter 5:8-9; 1 Timothy 2:1; 1 Thessalonians 5:8; 1 Thessalonians 5:17; Colossians 4:2; 1 John 5:4-5; Hebrews 4:12; Revelations 12:11

Confession:

I am strong in the Lord and in the power of His might. I put on the whole armor of God so that I am able to stand against the tricks of the enemy and endure in the days of trouble. I don't fight against people, but I fight against the spirits that cause the people's actions. I wear the belt of truth. I wear the breastplate of righteousness. I wear the shoes of peace. I use the shield of faith against those things that irritate me and distract me from God's will. I wear the helmet of salvation and I carry the sword of the Spirit, which is the Word of God. I pray always with all prayer and supplication in the spirit and I watch with all perseverance and supplication for all saints.

Meditating on the Promises of God

My thoughts:

Hebrews 11:6

But without faith it is impossible to please Him: for he that cometh to God must believe that He is, and that He is a rewarder of them that diligently seek Him.

Thoughts to Ponder:

- If I don't have faith, I can't please God.
- When I diligently seek God, His Word will guide me.
- Abraham's faith in God was counted to him as righteousness.

Also See:

Proverbs 3:5-6; Proverbs 8:17; Psalm 119:105; Romans 4:3

Meditating on the Promises of God

Confession:

Without faith it's impossible to please God. I believe that God exists, and He rewards me because I diligently seek Him.

My Thoughts:

_____

_____

_____

_____

_____

_____

Psalm 138:8

The Lord will perfect that which concerns me; Your mercy, O LORD, endures forever. Do not forsake the works of Your hands.

Thoughts to Ponder:

- I am the work of God's hands.
- God has a purpose and a plan for my life.
- God will finish what He started.

Also See:

Psalm 119:73; Isaiah 55:11; Jeremiah 29:11; Ephesians 2:10; Philippians 1:6

Confession:

The LORD will complete that which concerns me: the LORD's mercy lasts forever. He will not forsake (leave, forget about, neglect) the works of His hands.

My Thoughts:

1 Peter 5:6-7

6 Humble yourselves therefore under the mighty hand of God, that He may exalt you in due time: 7 Casting all your care upon Him; for He careth for you.

Psalm 55:22

Cast thy burden upon the LORD, and He shall sustain thee: He shall never suffer the righteous to be moved.

Thoughts to Ponder:

- Humility = Submission
- False Humility = Pride
- God didn't create me to carry burdens.
- The blood of Jesus has made me righteous.

Also See:

2 Chronicles 32:26; Proverbs 9:23; Psalm 27:13-14; Psalm 34:15; Psalm 37:5; Psalm 56:3-4; Isaiah 2:11; Matthew 6:31-34; Matthew 11:28-30; Luke 18:10-14; Philippians 4:6-7; Hebrews 13:5; 2 Corinthians 5:21

Confession:

I humble myself under the mighty hand of God and He exalts (promotes, prospers, increases, elevates) me in due time. I cast all my care upon Him because He cares for me and He sustains (keeps, provides for, strengthens) me. God will not allow the upright to be moved.

My Thoughts:

Matthew 11:28-30

28 Come unto me, all ye that labour and are heavy laden, and I will give you rest. 29 Take My yoke upon you and learn of me; for I am meek and lowly in heart: and ye shall find rest for your souls. 30 For My yoke is easy, and My burden is light.

Thoughts to Ponder:

- A yoke is used to lead and guide
- The yoke of Jesus is not burdensome or heavy. It doesn't cause hardships.
- When I study Jesus, I see how God wants me to conduct myself.

Also See:

Isaiah 48:17; Isaiah 55:1-3; Isaiah 61:1-4; Jeremiah 6:16; John 6:37; John 13:15; John 15:10-14; John 16:33; Galatians 5:1; Philippians 2:7-8; Philippians 4:13; 1 Peter 2:21-23; 1 John 5:3;

Confession:

When I go to Jesus because I am burdened down by the cares of the world. He will give me rest. I accept His guidance. I am studying (paying attention to) Him because He is humble and meek. In Jesus I find rest for my soul. His commands are easy and His requirements of me are light.

My Thoughts:

Isaiah 53:4-5

4 Surely, He hath borne our griefs, and carried our sorrows: yet we did esteem Him stricken, smitten of God, and afflicted. 5 But He was wounded for our transgressions, He was bruised for our iniquities: the chastisement of our peace was upon Him; and with His stripes we are healed.

Thoughts to Ponder:

- The price for sin is death.
- Jesus paid the price for my sin.
- I am healed because Jesus was beaten.

Also See:

Matthew 8:17; Matthew 20:28; 1 Peter 2:24-25; 1 Peter 3:18; Galatians 3:13; 2 Corinthians 5:21; 1 John 2:2

Confession:

Jesus was wounded for my transgressions; He was bruised for my iniquities. The purchase of my peace was upon Him and with His stripes I am healed.

My Thoughts:

Meditating on the Promises of God

1 Thessalonians 5:16-18

16 Rejoice evermore. 17 Pray without ceasing. 18 In every thing give thanks: for this is the will of God in Christ Jesus concerning you.

Thoughts to Ponder:

- Rejoicing is experiencing joy and gladness to a high degree.
- Prayer is communicating with God.
- Giving thanks is expressing gratitude or showing appreciation to someone.

My situations and circumstances should not determine my level of rejoicing, how often I pray, or when I give thanks to God. God has commanded that I do all three at all times.

Also See:

Matthew 5:12; Luke 18:1; Romans 12:12; Philippians 4:4; Philippians 4:6; Colossians 3:17; Colossians 4:12

Confession:

I rejoice evermore. I pray without ceasing. I give thanks in everything because this is the will of God in Christ Jesus concerning me.

My Thoughts:

Hebrews 13:5-6

5 Let your conversation be without covetousness; and be content with such things as ye have: for He hath saith, I will never leave thee, nor forsake thee. 6 So that we may boldly say, The Lord is my helper, and I will not fear what man shall do unto me.

Thoughts to Ponder:

- Desiring what others have distracts me from what God has for me.
- Desiring something isn't a bad thing, but my intent can cause the desire to be covetousness.
- As I seek God's kingdom and His righteousness, He will give me more than I can ever imagine.

Also See:

Psalm 37:25; Matthew 6:34; Luke 6:25-33; Luke 16:13-14; Romans 8:31; Hebrews 4:16; 1 Timothy 6:6-10; James 4:3

Confession:

My conversations are without covetousness and I am content with what I have because God will never leave me nor forsake me. I boldly say, "The LORD is my helper and I will not fear what man will do to me."

My Thoughts:

Proverbs 3:3-4

3 Let not mercy and truth forsake thee: bind them about thy neck; write them upon the table of thine heart:

4 So shalt thou find favour and good understanding in the sight of God and man.

Thoughts to Ponder:

- Mercy = Love
- Truth = God's Word
- God is love.

Also See:

Genesis 39:21; Joshua 1:7-8; Daniel 1:9; Psalm 25:10; Psalm 111:10; Psalm 119:27; Luke 2:41-52; John 3:16; Ephesians 5:1-2; Romans 4:18

Confession:

Mercy and truth does not forsake me; they are bound to my neck and written on my heart. I find favor and good understanding in the sight of God and man.

My Thoughts:

Philippians 4:19

But my God shall supply all your need according to His riches and glory by Christ Jesus.

Thoughts to Ponder:

- My wants aren't always the same as my needs.
- Needs are things that are necessary for me to live and to do the work that God has preordained me to do.
- My needs are not only financial, but spiritual, emotional, and physical.

Also See:

2 Samuel 22:7; Proverbs 3:9-10; Psalm 23; Psalm 84:11; Malachi 3:10; Micah 7:7; Luke 12:25-32; 1 Timothy 6:17; 1 Peter 5:10

Katie M. Littles

Confession:

God supplies all my needs according to His riches and glory by Christ Jesus.

My Thoughts:

2 Corinthians 57-58

57But thanks be to God, which giveth us the victory through our Lord Jesus Christ. 58 Therefore, my beloved brethren, be ye steadfast, immovable, always abounding in the work of the Lord, forasmuch as ye know that your labor is not in vain in the Lord.

Thoughts to Ponder:

- Opposition comes when we are doing God's will.
- We already have the victory because God ordained us to do the work.
- God's Word will not come back to Him void. It will do what He commands it to do.

Also See:

Isaiah 55:11; John 16:33; Ephesians 2:10; Ephesians 5:20; Philippians 4:4; 2 Corinthians 2:14; 1 John 5:4-7; 1 Thessalonians 5:18; Revelation 12:11

Confession:

I am steadfast and immovable. I'm always abounding in the work of the Lord. I know that my labor is not in vain in the Lord because God gives me victory through my Lord Jesus Christ.

My Thoughts:

1 John 4:4

***(KJV)** Ye are of God, little children, and have overcome them: because greater is He that is in you, than he that is in the world.*

***(MSG)** My dear children, you come from God and belong to God. You have already won a big victory over those false teachers, for the Spirit in you is stronger than anything in the world.*

Thoughts to Ponder:

- God created me in His image.
- I belong to God: He created me and then He purchased me with the Blood of Jesus.
- The Holy Spirit helps me.

Also See:

Genesis 1:26-27; John 3:16; John 14:16-17; John 14:20; John 14:26; John 15:7; John 15:18-19

Confession:

I am of God and have overcome the spirit of the antichrist because greater is the Spirit of God in me than he that is in the world.

My Thoughts:

Psalm 25:4-5

4 Shew me Thy ways, O LORD; teach me Thy paths. 5 Lead me in Thy truth, and teach me: for Thou art the God of my salvation; on Thee do I wait all the day long.

Thoughts to Ponder:

- God has a purpose and plan for my life.
- God's truth sanctifies me.
- God is the reason I am free from the yoke of sin.

Also See:

Proverbs 3:5-6; Psalm 86:11; Psalm 119:105; Psalm 119:27; Jeremiah 29:11; John 3:16; John 14:26; John 16:13; Ephesians 2:10

Confession:

Show me Your ways, O Lord; teach me Your paths. Lead me in Your truth and teach me: for You are the God of my salvation; on You, God, I wait all day.

My Thoughts:

Meditating on the Promises of God

Proverbs 3:5-8

*(**KJV**) 5 Trust in the LORD with all thine heart; and lean not unto thine own understanding. 6 In all thy ways acknowledge Him, and He shall direct thy paths. 7 Be not wise in thine own eyes: fear the LORD, and depart from evil. 8 It shall be health to thy navel, and marrow to thy bones.*

*(**NLT**) 5 Trust in the LORD with all your heart; do not depend on your own understanding. 6 Seek His will in all you do, and He will show you which path to take. 7 Don't be impressed with your own wisdom. Instead, fear the LORD and turn away from evil. 8 Then you will have healing for your body and strength for your bones.*

*(**MSG**) 5 Trust GOD from the bottom of your heart; don't try to figure out everything on your own. 6 Listen for GOD's voice in everything you do, everywhere you go; He's the one who will keep you on track. 7 Don't assume that you know it all. Run to GOD! Run from evil! 8 Your body will glow*

with health, and your very bones will vibrate with life!

Thoughts to Ponder:

- God already knows the paths He has for me, when I acknowledge Him, He shows me which way to go.
- God's wisdom is greater than my intellect.
- God's wisdom will always give me peace.

Also See:

Job 28:28; Proverbs 4:20-27; Proverbs 16:3; Proverbs 16:9; Proverbs 26:12; Psalm 32:8; Psalm 37:5; Isaiah 5:21; Isaiah 48:17; Jeremiah 17:7-8; Romans 12:16; Philippians 4:6; James 1:5

Confession:

I trust in the LORD with all my heart. I don't depend on my own understanding. I acknowledge God in everything I do; He directs my paths. I am not wise

Meditating on the Promises of God

in my own eyes. I stay away from evil; it is healing for my body and strength for my bones.

My Thoughts:

Isaiah 26:3-4

(KJV) 3 Thou wilt keep him in perfect peace, whose mind is stayed on Thee: because he trusteth in Thee. 4 Trust ye in the LORD for ever: for in the LORD JEHOVAH is everlasting strength: (KJV)

(AMP) 3 You will keep in perfect and constant peace the one whose mind is steadfast [that is, committed and focused on You – in both inclination and character], Because he trusts and takes refuge in You [with hope and confident expectation]. 4 Trust [confidently] in the LORD forever [He is your fortress, your shield, your banner]

Thoughts to Ponder:

- God gives me the ability to do what He created me to do.
- God's grace is His empowering presence to do what He has called me to do, to be who He has called me to be, and to have what He says I can have.

- God's presence gives me peace.

Also See:

Proverbs 3:5-6; Psalm 55:22; Psalm 62:11; Psalm 85:7-8; Isaiah 12:2; Jeremiah 17:7-8; John 14:27; John 16:33; Ephesians 2:10; Philippians 4:7; Philippians 4:13

Confession:

God keeps me in perfect peace and I am focused on Him because I trust in Him. I trust in the LORD forever because in the LORD JEHOVAH is everlasting strength.

My Thoughts:

Psalm 16:7-11 (MSG)

***7-8** The wise counsel GOD gives when I'm awake is confirmed by my sleeping heart. Day and night I'll stick with GOD; I've got a good thing going and I'm not letting go. **9-10** I'm happy from the inside out, and from the outside in, I'm firmly formed. You cancelled my ticket to hell – that's not my destination! **11** Now you've got my feet on the life path, all radiant from the shining of Your face. Ever since You took my hand, I'm on the right way.*

Thoughts to Ponder:

- Compare your life before Christ with your life after Christ. Are your levels of anxiety, stress, and anger better or worse?
- How many times have you reached out for help from a family member or friend and he/she weren't available or didn't have the resources to help?

- We owed a debt we couldn't pay; Jesus paid the debt for us by dying on the cross for our sins and transgressions.

Also See:

Psalm 4:7-8; Psalm 42:8; Psalm 62:6; Psalm 73:23; Isaiah 11:2-4; Jeremiah 29:11; John 3:16; Acts 2:8; Romans 8:11

Confession:

The wise counsel GOD gives when I'm awake is confirmed by my peaceful heart when I am asleep. I will stick with GOD day and night; I've got a good thing going and I'm not letting go. I'm happy from the inside out. I am firmly formed from the outside in. GOD cancelled my trip to hell – that's not my destination! God has me on the life path that's radiant from His shining face. Ever since He took my hand, I am on the right track.

Meditating on the Promises of God

My Thoughts:

John 14:1,27

1 Let not your heart be troubled: ye believe in God, believe also in me. 27 Peace I leave with you, My peace I give unto to: not as the world giveth, give I unto you. Let not your heart be troubled, neither let it be afraid.

Thoughts to Ponder:

- Stress affects your body, thoughts, feelings, and your behavior.
- Fear is an emotion that is excited by an expectation of evil or of something bad happening.
- The Holy Spirit is our comforter.

Also See:

Psalm 56:3; Isaiah 12:2-3; Isaiah 26:3; Isaiah 41:10; Jeremiah 1:8; John 14:26; John 16:33; Romans 8:6; Romans 15:13; Philippians 4:7; Colossians 3:15; 2 Corinthians 12:9; 2 Thessalonians 3:16; 2 Timothy 1:7

Confession:

I have the peace of Jesus. He left His peace with me; my heart is not troubled, nor afraid: I believe in God and I believe in Jesus.

My Thoughts:

Psalm 63:1-4 (MSG)

1 God – You're my God! I can't get enough of You! I've worked up such a hunger and thirst for God, traveling across dry and weary deserts. 2-4 So here I am in the place of worship, eyes open, drinking in Your strength and glory. In Your generous love I am really living at last! My lips brim praises like fountains. I bless You every time I take a breath; My arms wave like banners of praise to You.

Thoughts to Ponder:

- This Psalm was written by David when he was in the wilderness.
- The wilderness can be a lonely place; it can also be a place where we are able to draw closer to God because we are separated from people and distractions.
- Instead of thinking of the wilderness as a dry, deserted place, or a place of punishment, think of it as a place of restoration, renewal, and rebuilding.

Also See:

Exodus 15:2; Psalm 27:8; Psalm 42:1; Psalm 119:81; Psalm 143:10

Confession:

God, You're my God! I can't get enough of You! I've worked up such a hunger and a thirst for You, traveling across dry and weary deserts. So here I am in the place of worship, eyes open, drinking in Your strength and glory. In Your generous love I am really living at last! My lips brim praises like fountains. I bless You every time I take a breath. My arms wave like banners of praise to You.

My Thoughts:

Philippians 3:12-14

12 I'm not saying that I have this all together, that I have it made. But I am well on my way, reaching out for Christ, Who has so wondrously reached out for me. 13 Friends, don't get me wrong: By no means do I count myself an expert in all of this, but I've got my eye on the goal, where God is beckoning us onward – to Jesus. 14 I'm off and running, and I'm not turning back.

Thoughts to Ponder:

- As long as I'm on the earth, I have room to grow and mature in Christ.
- I'm not an expert in Christian living but I keep my focus on the One (Jesus) Who is.
- The great thing about this race is that we all win as long as we stay focused on Jesus.

Also See:

Luke 9:62; John 3:16; Ephesians 1:4; James 3:2; Philippians 1:6; Hebrews 6:1; Hebrews 12:1-2; Hebrews 13:21; 1 Peter 1:3-5; 2 Peter 3:18; 2 Timothy 4:7-8; 1 Thessalonians 2:12

Confession:

I don't have everything together; I don't have it made. But I am well on my way. I continually reach out for Christ because He has so wondrously reached out for me. Don't get me wrong, I don't consider myself to be an expert, but I do have my eye on the goal – onward to Jesus. I'm off and running and I'm not turning back.

Meditating on the Promises of God

My Thoughts:

2 Corinthians 5:17

Therefore, if any man be in Christ, he is a new creature: old things are passed away; behold, all things are become new.

Thoughts to Ponder:

- The old things that passed away when I came into Christ were my way of thinking, the way I reacted to people, situations, and the way I treated people.

- As I read, study, and meditate on God's Word, my mindset changes. My thoughts, actions, and words begin to align with God's Word.

Also See:

Psalm 51:10; Isaiah 43:18-19; Ezekiel 36:26; Romans 8:1; Romans 12:1-2; Ephesians 2:10; Ephesians 4:22-24; Philippians 2:5-8; Philippians 4:8; Colossians 3:1-10; Corinthians 5:21

Confession:

I am a new person because I am in Christ. Old things have passed away, all things have become new.

My Thoughts:

Galatians 5:22-23

22 But the fruit of the Spirit is love, joy, peace, longsuffering, gentleness, goodness, faith, 23 Meekness, temperance: against such there is no law.

Thoughts to Ponder:

- Jesus is the vine and I am a branch. My fruit is a direct result of my relationship with God.
- The closer I stay to Jesus, the more fruit of the Spirit I produce.
- It's possible to produce leaves and no fruit.

Also See:

Matthew 7:16-20; Matthew 21:18-19; John 15:5; John 15:16; Philippians 2:5; Philippians 4:8

Confession:

I produce the fruit of the Spirit: love, joy, peace, longsuffering, gentleness, goodness, faith, meekness, and temperance.

My Thoughts:

Isaiah 49:16

Behold, I have graven thee upon the palms of My hands; thy walls are continually before me.

Thoughts to Ponder:

- God will never forget about me.
- God sees my hard work.
- God has a plan for my life.

Also See:

Proverbs 16:3; Psalm 90:17; Jeremiah 29:11; Hebrews 13:5; Colossians 3:23-24; Philippians 2:14-15; Philippians 4:13; Galatians 6:9; 1 Corinthians 10:31

Confession:

My name is written on the palms of God's hands. The work I do is continually before Him.

Meditating on the Promises of God

My Thoughts:

Psalm 18:1-3

1 I will love Thee, O LORD, my strength.
2 The LORD is my rock, and my fortress, and my deliverer; my God, my strength, in Whom I will trust; my buckler, and the horn of my salvation, and my high tower. 3 I will call upon the LORD, Who is worthy to be praised: so shall I be saved from mine enemies.

Thoughts to Ponder:

- I don't fear because God is my protector.
- God is my place of safety.
- I can call upon God at any time.

Also See:

Proverbs 18:10; Psalm 19:14; Psalm 34:19; Psalm 118:14; Psalm 144:2; Psalm 145:3; Luke 1:67-75

Confession:

I love You, O LORD, my strength. The LORD is my rock and my fortress and my deliverer. The LORD is my God and my strength. I trust in Him. The LORD is my buckler and the horn of my salvation and my high tower. I call upon the LORD, Who is worthy to be praised, and I am saved from my enemies.

My Thoughts:

Psalm 27:1

The LORD is my light and salvation; whom shall I fear? The LORD is the strength of my life; of whom shall I be afraid?

Thoughts to Ponder:

- God gave me Jesus so that I could be rescued from eternal damnation.
- God gives me the strength I need when I am tired.
- God is for me; those against me will not succeed.

See Also:

Exodus 15:2; Psalm 32:8; Psalm 84:11; Psalm 119:105; Isaiah 40:29-31; Micah 7:7-8; John 3:16; John 8:12; Romans 8:31-34; 1 John 4:4; Revelation 21:23

Confession:

The LORD is my guide and my rescuer. The LORD is the strength of my life. Who should I fear? Who should I be afraid of?

My Thoughts:

Philippians 4:8

Finally, brethren, whatsoever things are pure, whatsoever things are lovely, whatsoever things are of good report; if there be any virtue, and if there be any praise, think on these things.

Thoughts To Ponder:

- Watch your thoughts, they become your words; watch your words, they become your actions; watch your actions, they become your habits; watch your habits, they become your character; watch your character, it becomes your destiny. (Lao Tzu – Chinese Philosopher)

See Also:

Ecclesiastes 10:20; Proverbs 15:1; Proverbs 15:28; Proverbs 17:27-28; Proverbs 18:21; Proverbs 21:23; Matthew 12:33-37; Matthew 15:11; Romans 8:5-6; Romans 12:2; Philippians 2:5; Philippians 4:6-7;

Colossians 3:2; 2 Corinthians 10:5; 1 Peter 1:13; 1 Peter 5:8; James 1:19

Confession:

I focus on things that are true, honest, just, pure, lovely and of good reports. I think about things that are excellent and worthy of praise.

My Thoughts:

Hebrews 12:1-3 (NLT)

***1** Therefore, since we are surrounded by such a huge crowd of witnesses to the life of faith, let us strip off every weight that slows us down, especially the sin that so easily trips us up. And let us run with endurance the race God has set before us. **2** We do this by keeping our eyes on Jesus, the champion who initiates and perfects our faith. Because of the joy awaiting Him, He endured the cross, disregarding its shame. Now He is seated in the place of honor beside God's throne. **3** Think of all the hostility He endured from sinful people; then you won't become weary and give up.*

Thoughts to Ponder:

- Our examples in faith are not only from the Bible. God surrounds us with people who are living faith-filled lives every day.
- If we keep our focus on Jesus, we will be able to finish this life strong. Study Him; see what He did and what He didn't do.

- We don't have to compete against each other because as a child of God, we should all have the same goal: eternal life in heaven.

Also See:

Micah 7:7; Luke 21:34-36; John 15:18-24; Romans 5:3-5; 2 Timothy 4:7; 1 Corinthians 9:24-27; 1 Corinthians 15:58; Ephesians 5:2; Galatians 6:9; Philippians 2:5-8; 2 Corinthians 7:1; Hebrews 6:15; Hebrews 10:35-39; 1 Peter 2:23-24; 1 Peter 3:18; Titus 2:13-14

Confession:

When I think about all Jesus endured, I don't become weary and give up. Because I am surrounded by people who live faith-filled lives, pleasing God. I rid myself of everything that slows me down, especially the sin that so easily trips me up and gets me off track. I run with endurance the race God has set before me by keeping my eyes on Jesus, the author and finisher of my faith.

My Thoughts:

Luke 10:19-20

***19** Behold, I give unto you power to tread on serpents and scorpions, and over all the power of the enemy: and nothing shall by any means hurt you. **20** Notwithstanding in this rejoice not, that the spirits are subject unto you; but rather rejoice, because your names are written in heaven.*

Thoughts to Ponder:

- I have the same power and authority that Jesus had when He was on the earth.

- Power is the faculty of doing or performing anything; the faculty of moving or of producing a change in something; ability or strength.

(Webster, Noah. American Dictionary of the English Language (1828 Edition) (Kindle Location 193647). Packard Technologies. Kindle Edition.)

Also See:

Psalm 91:13; Mark 16:18 Matthew 28:18-20; Acts 28:5; Romans 16:20

Confession:

I have power to tread on serpents and scorpions, and over all the power of the enemy: and nothing shall by any means hurt me. I rejoice because my name is written in heaven.

My Thoughts:

Colossians 3:17

And whatsoever ye do in word or deed, do all in the name of the Lord Jesus, giving thanks to God and the Father by Him.

Thoughts to Ponder:

- Do I consider whether or not I'm pleasing God when I am working, having conversations with others or just hanging out with friends?
- Working for God includes doing things outside the realm of the church building.
- God wants to be involved in everything I do, no matter how great or small.

Also See:

2 Chronicles 31:20-21; Proverbs 3:5-6; Micah 4:5; Romans 14:6-8; 1 Corinthians 10:13; Colossians 3:23; 1 Peter 2:9; 1 Peter 4:11; Hebrews 13:5; 1 Thessalonians 4:1-2

Confession:

Everything I do in word or deed, I do all in the name of the Lord Jesus, giving thanks to God the Father through Him.

My Thoughts:

Matthew 5:16

Let your light so shine before men, that they may see your good works, and glorify your Father which is in heaven.

Thoughts to Ponder:

- I am a light to the world.
- God created me to do good works.
- Some of these good works will put me in front of large audiences of people; I must remain humble in every area of my life.

Also See:

Isaiah 58:8; Isaiah 60:1-3; John 15:8; Matthew 5:14-15; Ephesians 2:10; Ephesians 5:8; Philippians 2:13-15; Colossians 3:17; 1 Peter 2:9;1 Timothy 6:17-19; 1 Peter 2:12; 1 Peter 3:15-16; 1 Peter 5:6; 2 Thessalonians 1:10-12;

Confession:

I let my light shine before men so they will see my good works and glorify my Father in heaven.

My Thoughts:

1 Corinthians 10:13

There hath no temptation taken you by such as is common to man: but God is faithful, who will not suffer you to be tempted above that ye are able; but will with the temptations also make a way of escape, that ye may be able to bear it.

Thoughts to Ponder:

- All temptation is from the devil; God does not tempt anyone.
- Because God is all-seeing, when the devil sends temptation my way, God provides an escape route for me.
- When I acknowledge God before I decide about anything, He will give me direction.

Also See:

Proverbs 3:5-6; Ephesians 6:12-13; James 1:13-14; 1 Peter 5:8-9; 1 Thessalonians 5:24; 2 Thessalonians 3:3

Confession:

I am not tempted by anything that other people haven't been tempted by. God is faithful, He will not allow me to be tempted beyond what I am able to resist. When the temptation comes, God also makes a way of escape for me so I will be able to bear it.

My Thoughts:

Romans 8:1-2

1There is therefore now no condemnation to them which are in Christ Jesus, who walk not after the flesh, but after the Spirit. 2 For the law of the Spirit of life in Christ Jesus hath made me free from the law of sin and death.

Thoughts to Ponder:

- Condemnation is from the devil and brings shame.
- Conviction is from God and leads to repentance.
- Walking after the flesh = agreeing with the devil.
- Walking after the Spirit = agreeing with God.

Also See:

John 3:18-19; Romans 4:7-8; Galatians 3:12; Galatians 5:16; 1 Corinthians 1:30; 2 Corinthians 5:17

Confession:

I am not condemned because I am in Christ Jesus. I walk according to the Spirit and not according to the flesh. The law of the Spirit of life in Christ Jesus has made me free from the law of sin and death.

My Thoughts:

1 Peter 1:2-4

2 Grace and peace be multiplied unto you through the knowledge of God, and of Jesus our Lord, 3 According as His divine power hath given us all things that pertain unto life and godliness, through the knowledge of Him that hath called us to glory and virtue: 4 Whereby are given unto us exceeding great and precious promises: that by these ye might be partakers of the divine nature, having escaped the corruption that is in the world through lust.

Thoughts to Ponder:

- God is His Word.
- God's Word gives me all I need to live a life of godliness.
- When I read God's Word, I am receiving first-hand information about God: who He is, what He likes, what He dislikes, and what He expects from men.

Also See:

Proverbs 3:5-6; John 1:1; John 15:4-5; John 15:15-16; Ephesians 1:7-12; Ephesians 1:18; 2 Thessalonians 2:13; 2 Peter 1:2; 1 John 2:29; 1 John 5:4; Colossians 1:27; 2 Timothy 4:8;

Confession:

Grace and peace are multiplied to me in the knowledge of God and of Jesus my Lord. God's divine power has given me all things that pertain to life and godliness through His knowledge (He has called me by glory and virtue). He has given me exceedingly great and precious promises so that I may be a partaker of the divine nature, having escaped the corruption that is in the world through lust.

Meditating on the Promises of God

My Thoughts:

Romans 8:29-32 (NLT)

***29** For God knew that His Son would be the firstborn among many brothers and sisters.*
***30** And having chosen them, He called them to come to Him. And having called them, He gave them right standing with Himself. And having given them right standing, He gave them His glory.*
31** What shall we say about such wonderful things as these? If God is for us, who can ever be against us?* ***32 *Since He did not spare even His own Son but gave Him up for us all, won't He also give us everything else?*

Thoughts to Ponder:

- God loves me.
- God chose me.
- God wants what is best for me.

Also See:

Genesis 15:1; Numbers 14:9; Psalm 56:4; Psalm 56:11; Psalm 118:6; Jeremiah 1:5; Isaiah 54:17; Jeremiah 1:19; Jeremiah 29:11; John 3:16; Romans 5:8-10; Romans 6:23; Ephesians 1:4-5; Ephesians 1:11; 2 Timothy 1:9; 1 Peter 2:9; 1 John 4:4; 1 Corinthians 2:12; 1 John 4:10

Confession:

God knew me in advance, and He chose me to become like Jesus. And having chosen me, He called me to come to Him. Having called me, He gave me right standing with Himself. Having given me right standing, He gave me His glory. God has done all these wonderful things for me. He wouldn't even spare Jesus, His own Son so, I know He will give me everything else. Because God is on my side, who could ever be against me?

My Thoughts:

1 Timothy 6:11-12

***11** But thou, O man of God, flee these things; and follow after righteousness, godliness, faith, love, patience, meekness. **12** Fight the good fight of faith, lay hold on eternal life, whereunto thou art also called, and hast professed a good profession before many witnesses.*

Thoughts to Ponder:

- When I accepted Jesus the Christ as my Lord and Savior, my way of living changed.
- I must turn away from the things that only satisfy my flesh.
- If I keep my eye on the prize of eternal life; I will be able to do all God has created me to do.

Also See:

Matthew 6:33; Galatians 5:19-23; Ephesians 6:10-18; 1 Corinthians 9:25-27; 1 Timothy 1:18-19; 2 Timothy 2:22; 2 Timothy 1:5-9; 2 Timothy 4:7-8; 1 Peter 1:5-7; 1 Peter 3:11; 1 Peter 5:10; 2 Peter 1:3; Philippians 4:8-9; 1 Corinthians 15:58; 2 Corinthians 5:17

Confession:

I am a man/woman of God. I run from evil things. I pursue righteousness and godly life, along with faith, love, perseverance, and gentleness. I fight the good fight for the true faith. I hold tightly to the eternal life to which God has called me, which I have declared so well before many witnesses.

My Thoughts:

Ephesians 4:1-3

(NASB) 1 Therefore I, the prisoner of the Lord, implore you to walk in a manner worthy of the calling with which you have been called, 2 with all humility and gentleness, with patience, showing tolerance for one another in love. 3 being diligent to preserve the unity of the Spirit in the bond of peace.

(NIV) 1 As the prisoner of the Lord, then, I urge you to live a life worthy of the calling you have received. 2 Be completely humble and gentle; be patient, bearing with one another in love. 3 Make every effort to keep the unity of the Spirit through the bond of peace.

Thoughts to Ponder:

- Before the foundation of the world was made, God had already chosen what He wanted you to do.

- Just as you have been created with a purpose so has everyone else in the world.

- Instead of being impatient with people, remember we all have been created for a certain person. Think about your journey as you navigate through life trying to figure out what you should and shouldn't do... everyone else faces the same thing.

Also See:

John 13:34; Romans 12:1; Romans 15:1; Ephesians 2:10; Ephesians 4:4; Philippians 1:27; Hebrews 12:14; 1 Thessalonians 2:12; 1 Thessalonians 4:1-2; 2 Thessalonians 1:11; 2 Peter 1:3; 2 Timothy 1:9; Colossians 3:12-13; 1 Corinthians 1:10; 1 Corinthians 12:12-13; 1 Corinthians 13:4-5; 1 Corinthians 13:7; 2 Corinthians 13:11; James 3:17-18

Confession:

I live a life that is worthy of the calling with which I have been called, with humility, gentleness, and patience. I show tolerance for others in love, being careful to preserve the unity of the Spirit in the bond of peace.

My Thoughts:

3 John 1:2 (NLT)

Dear friend, I hope all is well with you and that you are as healthy in body as you are strong in spirit.

Thoughts to Ponder:

- God desires that I be healthy naturally and spiritually.
- If I am unhealthy, I won't be able to fully do all God has determined me to do.
- If I don't know how to live a healthy life, God will give me the wisdom to do it.

Also See:

Proverbs 3:5-6; Isaiah 40:31; 2 Peter 1:3-9; 1 Corinthians 9:27

Confession:

All is well with me. I am as healthy in body as I am strong in spirit.

My Thoughts:

Galatians 5:1

Stand fast therefore in the liberty wherewith Christ hath made us free, and be not entangled again with the yoke of bondage.

Thoughts to Ponder:

- Liberty = Freedom
- Freedom = Not being enslaved Yoke of bondage = burdensome
- Yoke of Christ = light, not heavy, not burdensome

Also See:

Matthew 11:28-30; John 8:32-36; Hebrews 3:6; Hebrews 4:14; Romans 6:14; Romans 7:6; Romans 8:2; Galatians 4:9; Galatians 5:13; 1 Corinthians 15:58; 2 Corinthians 3:17; 1 Peter 2:16; 2 Peter 2:19

Confession:

I stand firm in the freedom with which Christ has made me free. I will not be entangled again with the yoke of bondage.

My Thoughts:

Psalm 57:7-11

7 My heart is fixed, O God, my heart is fixed: I will sing and give praise. 8 Awake up, my glory; awake, psaltery and harp: I myself will awake early. 9 I will praise Thee, O Lord, among the people: I will sing unto thee among the nations. 10 For Thy mercy is great unto the heavens, and Thy truth unto the clouds. 11 Be thou exalted, O God, above the heavens: let Thy glory be above all the earth.

Psalm 108:1-4

1 O God, my heart is fixed; I will sing and give praise, even with my glory. 2 Awake, psaltery and harp: I myself will awake early. 3 I will praise Thee, O Lord, among the people: and I will sing praises unto Thee among the nations. 4 For Thy mercy is great above the heavens: and Thy truth reaches unto the clouds.

Thoughts to Ponder:

- God's mercy is everlasting, and His truth endures forever.

- I will glorify God every chance I get. This includes through my words and actions.
- God never changes; He is the same yesterday, today, and forever.

Also See:

Proverbs 8:17; Psalm 36:5; Psalm 71:19; Psalm 85:10-11; Psalm 96:10; Psalm 103:11; Psalm 112:7; Psalm 113:4; Psalm 138:4-5; Isaiah 40:8; Isaiah 52:9; Matthew 24:35; Ephesians 5:20; Hebrews 13:8

Confession:

My heart is fixed, my heart is fixed. I will sing and give praise. I praise God among the people. I sing to God among the nations. God's mercy reaches to the heavens and His truth unto the clouds. God is exalted above the heavens. God's glory is above all the earth.

My Thoughts:

1 Peter 1:13-16 (NIV)

***13** Therefore, with minds that are alert and fully sober, set your hope on the grace to be brought to you when Jesus Christ is revealed at His coming. **14** As obedient children, do not conform to the evil desires you had when you lived in ignorance. **15** But just as He Who called you is holy, so be holy in all you do; **16** for it is written: "Be holy, because I am holy."*

Thoughts to Ponder:

- If I consistently read God's Word, my mind will remain clear and alert.
- God's Spirit lives inside of me, therefore I can be holy.
- Before I accepted Jesus the Christ as my Lord and Savior, I lived in ignorance.

Also See:

Luke 12:35; John 15:4-5; Ephesians 5:1-2; 1 Peter 4:7; Romans 12:2; Philippians 1:27; 1 Peter 2:9-12; 1 Peter 3:15; 1 Peter 5:8; 1 John 4:4; 2 Timothy 1:7; Titus 2:11-13

Confession:

My mind is alert and fully sober; my hope is set on the grace to be brought to me when Jesus Christ is revealed at His coming. Because I am an obedient child of God, I do not conform to the sinful desires I had before I came into the knowledge of the truth of Christ. God is holy; because He has called me, I am also holy in all I do.

My Thoughts:

Psalm 119:105

Thy word is a lamp unto my feet, and a light unto my path.

Thoughts to Ponder:

- God has already planned the paths for my life.

- If I stay in His word, I will see my life paths.

- If I make a wrong turn, God will guide me back to the path through His word.

Also See:

Proverbs 6:20-23; Isaiah 55:7; Jeremiah 1:5; Jeremiah 29:11; Joel 2:3; Zechariah 1:3; James 4:8

Confession:

God's Word is a lamp unto my feet, and a light unto my path.

My Thoughts:

Meditating on the Promises of God

Psalm 73:24,26,28

***24** Thy shalt guide me with thy counsel, and afterward receive me to glory. **26** My flesh and my heart fail: but God is the strength of my heart, and my portion forever. **28** But it is good for me to draw near to God: I have put my trust in the Lord GOD, that I may declare all thy works.*

Thoughts to Ponder:

- God did not put me on the earth for me to walk around aimlessly from day to day. He already has my journey planned out.

- When I feel like giving up, God will strengthen me to continue doing the work He has assigned me.

Also See:

Lamentations 3:25-26; Proverbs 3:5-6; Psalm 16:5-6; Psalm 18:2; Psalm 25:9; Psalm 32:8; Psalm 118:17; Psalm 119:105; Isaiah 40:28-31; Isaiah 48:17; Isaiah 58:11; Matthew 6:25-34; James 1:5; Hebrews 10:19-22; 2 Corinthians 4:16-18; James 4:8; 2 Corinthians 12:9-10;

Confession:

God guides me with counsel and afterward receives me to glory. God is the strength of my heart, and my portion forever. It is good for me to draw near to God: I have put my trust in the Lord GOD, that I may declare all His works.

My Thoughts:

Ephesians 3:20

*(**KJV**) Now unto Him that is able to do exceeding abundantly above all that we ask or think, according to the power that worketh in us.*

*(**NLT**) Now all glory to God, Who is able, through His mighty power at work within us, to accomplish infinitely more than we might ask or think.*

Thoughts to Ponder:

- God can and will do more for me than my mind can imagine.
- Whatever I think is more than enough, God can and will do more than that.
- Because His power is inside of me, I am able to do all that God wants me to do even though it may seem to be an unattainable task in my sight.

Also See:

Genesis 18:10-14; Daniel 6:16-22; Jeremiah 32:27; John 10:10; Ephesians 1:19; Philippians 4:13; 1 Corinthians 2:9; 2 Corinthians 9:8; 1 John 4:4

Confession:

All glory to God, Who is able, through His mighty power at work within me, is able to do beyond abundantly above all I could ever ask or think.

My Thoughts:

Philippians 4:4-7

(KJV) 4 Rejoice in the Lord always: and again, I say, Rejoice. 5 Let your moderation be known unto all men. The Lord is at hand. 6 Be careful for nothing: but in everything by prayer and supplication with thanksgiving let your requests be made known to God. 7 And the peace of God, which passes all understanding, shall keep your hearts and minds through Christ Jesus.

(NIV) 4 Rejoice in the Lord always. I will say it again: Rejoice! 5 Let your gentleness be evident to all. The Lord is near. 6 Do not be anxious about anything, but in every situation, by prayer and petition, with thanksgiving, present your requests to God. 7 And the peace of God, which transcends all understanding, will guard your hearts and your minds in Christ Jesus.

Thoughts to Ponder:

- Worry and anxiety are symptoms of fear.
- Fear is a strategy of the devil to keep me from moving forward.
- Even when things are not going the way I think or want them to go, I will rejoice in (give thanks to, glorify) God.

Also See:

Psalm 34:5-7; Psalm 55:22; Psalm 62:8; Proverbs 3:5-6; Proverbs 16:3; Isaiah 26:3; Matthew 6:25-33; Matthew 7:7-8; John 14:27; Romans 12:12; 1 Thessalonians 5:16-18; Colossians 4:2; Colossians 3:15-17; 1 Peter 4:7; 1 Peter 5:7; 2 Timothy 1:7

Confession:

I rejoice in the Lord always. I let my gentleness be evident to all. The Lord is near. I am not anxious about anything, but in every situation by prayer and petition, with thanksgiving, I present my requests to God. The peace of God, which goes beyond all understanding, guards my heart and my mind in Christ Jesus.

My Thoughts:

Ecclesiastes 3:17

I said in mine heart, God shall judge the righteous and the wicked: for there is a time there for every purpose and for every work.

Thoughts to Ponder:

- God is the judge of everyone.
- There is a time and a purpose for everything that is done in the earth.
- All things work together for my good.

Also See:

Ecclesiastes 3:1; Ecclesiastes 12:14; Psalm 98:8-9; Romans 2:5-10; Romans 8:28; 2 Corinthians 5:10

Confession:

God shall judge the righteous and the wicked because there is a time and purpose for every work.

My Thoughts:

Jeremiah 33:3

Call unto me, and I will answer thee, and shew thee great and mighty things, which thou knowest not.

Thoughts to Ponder:

- God wants me to call to Him.
- God is ready to give me the answers I need.
- God wants to show me great and mighty things; things I could never imagine.

Also See:

Deuteronomy 4:29; 2 Chronicles 7:14-16; Proverbs 3:5-6; Psalm 91:15; Psalm 145:18; Isaiah 55:6-7; Isaiah 65:24; Jeremiah 29:12; Luke 11:9-10; Acts 2:21; Ephesians 3:20

Confession:

When I call on the Lord, He answers me and shows me great and mighty things which I don't know.

My Thoughts:

Romans 12:3

For I say, through the grace given unto me, to every man that is among you, not to think of himself more highly than he ought to think; but to think soberly, according as God hath dealt to every man the measure of faith.

Ephesians 2:8-10

***8** For by grace are ye saved through faith; and that not of yourselves: it is the gift of God: **9** Not of works, lest any man should boast. **10** For we are His workmanship, created in Christ Jesus unto good works, which God hath before ordained that we should walk in them.*

Thoughts to Ponder:

- In God, everyone starts out on an even plane. I am no better or less than anyone else no matter what title or position I hold.

- Salvation is a free gift that God gave the world. The only way for me to receive it is through believing in Christ Jesus.

- Part of my purpose is to do the good works God assigns me to do.

Also See:

Ecclesiastes 7:16; Proverbs 16:18-19; Proverbs 26:12; Romans 12:16; John 3:16; Galatians 6:3; Philippians 3:3-8; 1 Peter 4:7; 1 Peter 5:5; 1 Corinthians 7:17; 1 Corinthians 12:7-11

Confession:

I don't think of myself more highly than I should; I think with a level head according to the measure of faith God has given to me. I am saved by grace and not by works. Grace is a gift from God. I am God's workmanship created in Christ Jesus to do good works which He has prepared in advance as my way of life.

My Thoughts:

1 Samuel 15:22-23a

22 And Samuel said, Hath the LORD as great delight in burnt offerings and sacrifices, as in obeying the voice of the LORD? Behold, to obey is better than sacrifice, and to hearken than the fat of rams. 23a For rebellion is as the sin of witchcraft, and stubbornness is as iniquity and idolatry.

Thoughts to Ponder:

- Obeying God is better than a sacrificial offering. Rebellion = Witchcraft
- Stubbornness= Sin and Idolatry

Also See:

Hosea 6:6; Proverbs 21:3; Psalm 51:16-17; Jeremiah 7:22-23; Micah 6:6-8; Matthew 9:13; Matthew 12:7; Mark 12:33

Confession:

Rebellion is as the sin of witchcraft and being stubborn is the same as sin and idol worship. I will obey the voice of God because He is more pleased with obedience than He is with offerings and sacrifices.

My Thoughts:

Isaiah 1:19

If ye be willing and obedient, ye shall eat the good of the land

Thoughts to Ponder:

- I must desire to do what God has instructed me to do.
- Everything I do for God is with a willing heart.
- When I obey God in small things, He will open the door for bigger things.

Also See:

Deuteronomy 30:15-16; 1 Samuel 23a; 1 Kings 9:1-5; Psalm 37:4; Isaiah 3:10; Matthew 21:28-32; Matthew 25:14-29

Confession:

I eat the good of the land because I am willing and obedient to God.

My Thoughts:

James 1:5-8

5 If any of you lack wisdom, let him ask of God, that giveth to all men liberally, and upbraideth not; and it shall be given him, 6 But let him ask in faith, nothing wavering. For he that wavereth is like a wave of the sea driven with the wind and tossed. 7 For let not that man think that he shall receive any thing of the Lord. 8 A double minded man is unstable in all his ways.

Thoughts to Ponder:

- God's wisdom is better than my intellect.
- God will not withhold any good thing from me if I ask in faith.
- I can only please God if I have faith. He wants me to ask for things that seem to be unattainable.

Also See:

1 Kings 3:7-12; 2 Chronicles 1:10; Proverbs 2:3-6; Proverbs 3:5-7; Jeremiah 29:12-13; Matthew 7:7-11; John 15:7; 1 John 5:14-15; John 16:23-24; Hebrews 11:6; James 3:17; 2 Timothy 1:7

Confession:

When I lack wisdom, I ask God for it. He gives it to me freely and without hesitation. I ask in faith, not doubting because I am not like a wave of the sea driven and tossed by the wind; I am not double-minded nor am I unstable in all my ways.

My Thoughts:

2 Timothy 2:23-26 (NLT)

23 Again I say, don't get involved in foolish, ignorant arguments that only start fights. 24 A servant of the Lord must not quarrel but must be kind to everyone, be able to teach, and be patient with difficult people. 25 Gently instruct those who oppose the truth. Perhaps God will change those people's hearts, and they will learn the truth. 26 Then they will come to their senses and escape from the devil's trap. For they have been held captive by him to do whatever he wants.

Thoughts to Ponder:

- Because I am in Christ Jesus, I no longer engage in arguments with others. That will only start fights.

- I choose to remain humble. My humility will open the door for me to give a reason for why I believe what I believe.

- God is the one who changes the hearts of unbelievers; I am just a vessel made available to be used by Him.

Also See:

Philippians 2:3; Colossians 3:13; 1 Timothy 2:1-4; 1 Timothy 6:11; 2 Timothy 2:14; 2 Timothy 2:16; James 1:19-20; Titus 1:6-9; Titus 3:9

Confession:

I don't get involved in foolish, ignorant arguments that only start fights. As a servant of the Lord, I don't quarrel, but I am kind to everyone, I am able to teach, and I am patient with difficult people. I gently instruct those who oppose the Truth because there's a chance God will change their hearts and they will learn the Truth. Then they will come to their senses and escape from the devil's trap that keeps them in captivity doing what he wants them to do.

My Thoughts:

Romans 4:17

(KJV) *(As it is written, I have made thee a father of many nations,) before him whom he believed, even God, who quickeneth the dead, and calleth those things which be not as though they were.*

(MSG) *We call Abraham "father" not because he got God's attention by living like a saint, but because God made something out of Abraham when he was a nobody. Isn't that what we've always read in Scripture, God saying to Abraham, "I set you up as a father of many peoples"? Abraham was first named "father" and then became a father because he dared to trust God to do what only God could do: raise the dead to life, with a word made something out of nothing.*

Thoughts to Ponder:

- I shall have what I say I have.
- I speak the things I want to see.

- God called Abraham a father when he didn't have any children.
- Nothing is impossible if I believe God.

Also See:

Genesis 15:1-6; Genesis 17:1-7; Job 42:2; Proverbs 3:5-6; Psalm 37:4; Isaiah 40:29; Isaiah 41:10; Jeremiah 32:27; Luke 1:37; Matthew 19:26; Mark 11:22-24; Romans 8:28; Philippians 4:6; Philippians 4:13; Philippians 4:19; Hebrews 4:16; Hebrews 11:1-3; Hebrews 11:6; 1 John 5:4

Confession:

I speak things into existence because I trust God to do what only God can do: raise the dead to life, with a word, make something out of nothing.

My Thoughts:

Psalm 121 (NLT)

***1** I look up to the mountains – does my help come from there? **2** My help comes from the LORD, Who made heaven and earth! **3** He will not let you stumble; the One Who watches over you will not slumber, **4** Indeed, He Who watches over Israel never slumbers or sleeps. **5** The LORD Himself watches over you! The LORD stands beside you as your protective shade. **6** The sun will not harm you by day, nor the moon at night. **7** The LORD keeps you from all harm and watches over your life. **8** The LORD keeps watch over you as you come and go, both now and forever.*

Thoughts to Ponder:

- God is an ever present help in time of trouble.
- God is constantly watching over me.

Also See:

Genesis 1:1; Deuteronomy 28:6; Proverbs 2:8; Proverbs 3:5-6; Psalm 27:1; Psalm 34:22; Psalm 41:2; Psalm 91:1; Psalm 91:5-12; Psalm 124:8; Isaiah 27:3; Isaiah 40:28-29; Isaiah 41:13; Hebrews 13:6; 2 Timothy 4:18

Confession:

Does my help come from the mountains that I look to? My help comes from the LORD, Who made heaven and earth! He will not let me stumble; God watches over me and He never sleeps. The LORD Himself watches over me. He stands beside me as my protector. The LORD keeps me from all harm and watches over my life as I come and go, now and forever.

My Thoughts:

1 Corinthians 2:9

But as it is written, Eye hath not seen, nor ear heard, neither have entered into the heart of man, the things which God hath prepared for them that love Him.

Thoughts to Ponder:

- God has things prepared for me that my mind cannot imagine.
- As I draw closer to God and seek His face more and the more I obey His commands then He will begin to give me more and more 'impossible' assignments.
- I don't think it strange when I have thoughts of things that seem impossible.
- I can do all things through Christ, Who strengthens me.

Also See:

2 Chronicles 7:14-16; Proverbs 8:12; Psalm 24:1-6; Psalm 27:4; Isaiah 43:18-19; Isaiah 55:6; Isaiah 64:4-5a; Jeremiah 33:3; Matthew 6:33; Matthew 7:7-8; Luke 11:9-10; Acts 17:24-28; Romans 8:28; Philippians 4:13; Hebrews 11:6; Ephesians 2:10; James 2:5; James 4:8

Confession:

No eye has seen, no ear has heard, and no mind has imagined what God has prepared for me because I love Him.

My Thoughts:

1 Peter 5:8-10

(KJV) 8 Be sober, be vigilant; because your adversary the devil, as a roaring lion, walketh about, seeking whom he may devour. 9 Whom resist steadfast in the faith, knowing that the same afflictions are accomplished in your brethren that are in the world. 10 But the God of all grace, who hath called us unto His eternal glory by Christ Jesus, after that ye have suffered a while, make you perfect, stablish, strengthen, settle you.

(NLT) 8 Stay alert! Watch out for your great enemy, the devil. He prowls around like a roaring lion, looking for someone to devour. 9 Stand firm against him and be strong in your faith. Remember that your family of believers all over the world is going through the same kind of suffering you are. 10 In his kindness God called you to share in His eternal glory by means of Christ Jesus. So after you have suffered a little while, He will restore, support, and strengthen you, and will place you on a firm foundation.

Thoughts to Ponder:

- The devil is a bully pretending to be something he is not.
- I have power and authority over the devil.
- If you resist the devil he will flee.

Also See:

Matthew 10:1; Mark 6:7; Luke 9:1; Luke 10:19; Romans 12:1-2; Romans 16:20; Ephesians 4:22-27; Ephesians 6:11-18; James 1:13-14; James 4:7; Philippians 4:13; 1 John 2:13; 1 Peter 1:13; 1 Corinthians 10:13; Revelation 20:10

Confession:

I am alert, I am vigilant because my enemy, the devil, walks around like a roaring lion, seeking whom he can trip up. I resist him because I stand firm in God's Word. I know that my family of believers all over the world are going through the same kind of suffering I am.

Meditating on the Promises of God

My Thoughts:

Psalm 34:8-10

8 O taste and see that the LORD is good: blessed is the man that trusteth in Him. 9 O fear the LORD, ye His saints: for there is no want to them that fear Him. 10 The young lions do lack, and suffer hunger: but they that seek the LORD shall not want for any good thing.

Thoughts to Ponder:

- To fear the LORD means to reverence, honor, and respect Him.
- To taste and see is the same as having an encounter with God, believing and trusting His Word, and experiencing His Word manifesting in my life.
- As long as I seek God, He will not withhold any good thing from me.

Also See:

Leviticus 20:26; Proverbs 3:5-6; Psalm 23:1; Psalm 52:1; Psalm 84:11; Psalm 119:103; Isaiah 43:1; Jeremiah 31:14; Luke 12:30-32; John 17:6; Philippians 4:19; 1 Peter 2:2-3; 1 Corinthians 3:23

Confession:

Taste and see that the LORD is good! I am blessed because I take refuge in Him. I fear the LORD because I am His saint and I lack nothing. Young lions go lacking and hungry but I lack no good thing because I seek the LORD.

My Thoughts:

Psalm 62:5-8

5 My soul, wait thou only upon God; for my expectation is from Him. 6 He only is my rock and my salvation: He is my defense; I shall not be moved. 7 In God is my salvation and my glory: the rock of my strength, and my refuge, is in God. 8 Trust in Him at all times; ye people, pour out your heart before Him: God is a refuge for us. Selah.

Thoughts to Ponder:

- I am a spiritual being, I live in a body, and I have a soul
- My soul includes my mind, my will and my emotions.
- Once I get my soul to agree with my spirit then it's easy for me to wait on God.

Also See:

Genesis 1:26-27; Genesis 2:7; Micah 7:7; Psalm 16:8; Psalm 18:31-32; Psalm 27:13-14; Isaiah 45:17; Lamentations 3:24-26; John 6:67-69; 1 Corinthians 1:30-31; Philippians 4:6; 1 Thessalonians 5:23; Hebrews 4:12

Confession:

My soul (my mind, my will, and my emotions), wait upon God; because my expectation is from Him. He only is my rock and my salvation and my glory: the rock of my strength, and my refuge, is in God. I trust in Him at all times; I pour out my heart before Him. God is a refuge for me. Selah.

Meditating on the Promises of God

My Thoughts:

Psalm 27:8, 11-14

8 When Thou saidst, Seek ye My face; my heart said unto Thee, Thy face, LORD, will I seek. 11 Teach me Thy way, O LORD, and lead me in a plain path, because of mine enemies. 12 Deliver me not over unto the will of mine enemies: for false witnesses are risen up against me, and such as breathe out cruelty. 13 I had fainted, unless I had believed to see the goodness of the LORD in the land of the living. 14 Wait on the LORD: be of good courage, and He shall strengthen thine heart: wait, I say on the LORD.

Thoughts to Ponder:

- God desires a relationship with me. His love for me didn't stop at Jesus dying for my sins.
- Life gets hard sometimes, but I won't give up because God has a purpose and a plan for me.
- When I feel like giving up, I can ask God to give me the strength to go on.

Also See:

Nehemiah 8:10; Hosea 5:15; Proverbs 2:6-9; Psalm 5:8; Psalm 3:5-6; Psalm 25:4-5; Psalm 42:1; Psalm 63:1-2; Psalm 86:11; Psalm 119:10; Psalm 119:105; Isaiah 55:6-7; Jeremiah 29:11-13; John 3:16; Galatians 6:9; Ephesians 2:10; 1 Corinthians 5:58

Confession:

My heart said, "Seek His face". Your face O LORD, I will seek. The LORD teaches me and leads me on a level path, because of my oppressors. He does not hand me over to the will of my enemies, for false witnesses rise up against me, breathing out violence. I am certain to see the goodness of the LORD in the land of the living. I wait patiently for the LORD. I am strong and courageous. I wait patiently for the LORD!

My Thoughts:

Psalm 34:1-7

1 I will bless the LORD at all times: His praise shall continually be in my mouth. 2 My soul shall make her boast in the LORD: the humble shall hear thereof, and be glad. 3 O magnify the LORD with me, and let us exalt His name together. 4 I sought the LORD, and He heard me, and delivered me from all my fears. 5 They look unto Him, and were lightened: and their faces were not ashamed. 6 This poor man cried, and the LORD heard him, and saved Him out of all his troubles. 7 The angel of the LORD encamps round about them that fear Him, and delivers them.

Thoughts to Ponder:

- God is worthy to be praised.
- Not only did God give me the gift of salvation, He protects me and delivers me out of all my troubles.

Also See:

2 Kings 6:15-17; Daniel 6:22; Psalm 23:4; Psalm 71:14-15; Psalm 91:11; Psalm 116:1-6; Isaiah 12:2; Jeremiah 29:4; Ephesians 5:20; 1 Thessalonians 5:18; Colossians 3:17; 1 Corinthians 1:30-31; 2 Corinthians 10:17; Matthew 7:7; Luke 1:39-46; 2 Timothy 1:7

Confession:

I will bless the LORD at all times; His praise will always be on my lips. My soul boasts in the LORD; let the oppressed hear and rejoice. Magnify the LORD with me! I sought the LORD, and He answered me; He delivered me from all my fears. I am radiant with joy because I look to Him! My face will never be ashamed. I called out, and the LORD heard me; He saved me from all my troubles. The angel of the LORD encamps around me because I fear Him and He delivers me.

My Thoughts:

Philippians 1:27-29 (NLT)

27 Above all, you must live as citizens of heaven, conducting yourselves in a manner worthy of the Good News about Christ. Then, whether I come and see you again or only hear about you, I will know that you are standing together with one spirit and one purpose, fighting together in the faith, which is the Good News. 28 Don't be intimidated in any way by your enemies. This will be a sign to them that they are going to be destroyed, but that you are going to be saved, even by God Himself. 29 For you have been given not only the privilege of trusting in Christ by also the privilege of suffering for Him.

Thoughts to Ponder:

- I live on the earth, but I am a citizen of the Kingdom of Heaven.

- The laws that govern the Kingdom of Heaven are not the same as the laws that govern earthly realms.

- The Bible (God's Word) is the governing authority of Heaven.

Also See:

Isaiah 51:7; Matthew 5:10-12; Acts 5:41; Acts 14:22; Romans 1:16; Romans 5:3-5; Romans 8:14-17; Ephesians 4:1-6; Philippians 2:1-2; Hebrews 13:6; 1 Corinthians 1:10; 1 Corinthians 16:13-14; 1 Thessalonians 3:12-4:7; 1 Peter 4:12-14; 2 Timothy 1:7-8; 2 Timothy 2:11-12; James 1:2-4

Confession:

Above all I live as a kingdom citizen of heaven, conducting myself in a manner worthy of the Good News about Christ. Whether others see me or only hear about me, they will know that I am standing with my fellow co-laborers in Christ with one spirit and one purpose, fighting together for the faith, which is the Good News. I am not intimidated in any way by my enemies. This is a sign to them that they are going to be destroyed, but I am going to be saved, even by God Himself because I have been given not only the privilege of trusting in Christ but also the privilege of suffering for Him.

My Thoughts:

2 Corinthians 10:3-6

3 For though we walk in the flesh, we do not war after the flesh: 4 (For the weapons of our warfare are not carnal, but mighty through God to the pulling down of strong holds;) 5 Casting down imaginations, and every high thing that exalts itself against the knowledge of God, and bringing into captivity every thought to the obedience of Christ. 6 And having in a readiness to revenge all disobedience, when your obedience is fulfilled.

Thoughts to Ponder:

- I can't fight spiritual battles with physical weapons; I have to use spiritual weapons.
- My spiritual weapons are prayer and principles found in God's Word.

Also See:

Joshua 6; Judges 15:10-14; 1 Samuel 17:45-50; Zechariah 4:6; Isaiah 1:16-20; Matthew 11:29-30; Ephesians 6:12-18; Romans 8:1-6; Hebrews 4:12; 1 Corinthians 2:1-5; 1 Corinthians 3:18-19; 2 Corinthians 4:7; 1 Peter 1:14-15

Confession:

I am human but I don't fight according to human ways. For the weapons of my warfare cannot be seen but they are mighty in God (spiritual) for pulling down strongholds, casting down arguments and every high thing that exalts itself against the knowledge of God, bringing every thought into captivity to the obedience of Christ, and being ready to punish all disobedience when my obedience is fulfilled.

Meditating on the Promises of God

My Thoughts:

1 Corinthians 3:16

Know ye not that ye are the temple of God, and that the Spirit of God dwelleth in you?

Thoughts to Ponder:

- God's Spirit lives in me.
- Because God's Spirit lives in me, I am able to live according to the Spirit and not according to the flesh.

Also See:

Genesis 1:26; Ezekiel 36:27; Ezekiel 37:14; John 14:14-20; Acts 1:8; Romans 8:1-6; Romans 8:9-11; 1 Corinthians 16:19-20; 2 Corinthians 6:16; 2 Timothy 1:13-14; 1 John 4:4; 1 John 4:11-15; 1 Peter 1:16;

Confession:

I am God's temple; God's Spirit lives in me.

My Thoughts:

2 Peter 3:9 (NLT)

The Lord isn't really being slow about His promise, as some people think. No, He is being patient for your sake. He does not want anyone to be destroyed, but wants everyone to repent.

Thoughts to Ponder:

- Some of God's promises require that I achieve a certain level of maturity so that I won't misuse/mistreat the promise and destroy myself.

- Sometimes the promises of God are slow in coming because the promise made to you is directly connected with the promise made to someone else.

Also See:

Isaiah 30:18; Habakkuk 2:3; Luke 1:5-20; Luke 1:60-80; John 1:6-8

Confession:

God will fulfill every promise He made. He is being patient for my sake. He does not want me to be destroyed.

My Thoughts:

Ephesians 5:15-20 (NLT)

15 So be careful how you live. Don't live like fools, but like those who are wise. 16 Make the most of every opportunity in these evil days. 17 Don't act thoughtlessly, but understand what the Lord wants you do. 18 Don't be drunk with wine, because that will ruin your life. Instead, be filled with the Holy Spirit, 19 singing psalms and hymns and spiritual songs among yourselves, and making music to the Lord in your hearts. 20 And give thanks for everything to God the Father in the name of our Lord Jesus Christ.

Thoughts to Ponder:

- When I acknowledge God in everything I do, I am carefully considering all my actions.
- God will give me wisdom if I ask for it.

Also See:

Job 28:28; Proverbs 3:5-6; Proverbs 3:20-21; Proverbs 14:8; Proverb 20:1; Psalm 16:11; Psalm 111:10; Psalm 119:105; Isaiah 5:22; Acts 16:25-26; Luke 21:34; John 12:35; Romans 12:2; Ephesians 6:13; Colossians 1:9-13; Colossians 3:16-17; Colossians 4:5; 1 Corinthians 14:26; Philippians 1:27; James 1:5; James 3:13; 1 Thessalonians 5:18; Hebrews 13:15-16

Confession:

I am careful how I live. I live wisely, not like a fool. I make the most of every opportunity in these evil days. I don't act thoughtlessly but I understand what the Lord wants me to do. I don't get drunk but instead I am filled with the Holy Spirit, and sing psalms, hymns, and spiritual songs with my brothers and sisters. I make music to the Lord in my heart. I give thanks for everything to God the Father in the name of my Lord Jesus the Christ.

My Thoughts:

2 Corinthians 2:14–17 (NLT)

***14** But thank God! He has made us His captives and continues to lead us along in Christ's triumphal procession. Now He uses us to spread the knowledge of Christ everywhere, like a sweet perfume. **15** Our lives are a Christ-like fragrance rising up to God. But this fragrance is perceived differently by those who are being saved and by those who are perishing. **16** To those who are perishing, we are a dreadful smell of death and doom. But to those who are being saved, we are a life-giving perfume. And who is adequate for such a task as this? **17** You see, we are not like the many hucksters who preach for personal profit. We preach the word of God with sincerity and with Christ's authority, knowing that God is watching us.*

Thoughts to Ponder:

- When others see me, they see Christ.
- I have the ability to change the atmosphere (the tone) of any place, situation, or circumstance because the Holy Spirit lives on the inside of me.

Also See:

Romans 6:17; Acts 20:19-28; Romans 8:37; Ephesians 5:2; Colossians 2:10-15; 1 Corinthians 1:18; 1 Corinthians 5:8; 2 Corinthians 1:12; 2 Corinthians 3:5-6; 2 Corinthians 4:2-4; 1 Peter 2:7-8;

Confession:

But thank God! He has made me His captive and continues to lead me along in Christ's triumphal procession. Now He uses me to spread the knowledge of Christ everywhere, like a sweet perfume. My life is a Christ-like fragrance rising up to God. But this fragrance is perceived differently by those who are perishing. To those who are perishing,

I am a dreadful smell of doom. But to those who are being saved, I am a life giving perfume. I am not like a peddler who preaches for personal gain. I preach the Word of God with sincerity and with Christ's authority, knowing God is watching me.

My Thoughts:

I'd LOVE to hear from you!

Please share how, *Meditating on the Promises of God,* has impacted your life by leaving a review on Amazon.

www.ingramcontent.com/pod-product-compliance
Lightning Source LLC
Chambersburg PA
CBHW021058080526
44587CB00010B/293